my PLANET EARTH Infographic sticker Activity BOOK

Activity stickers, and extra ones to use anywhere in the book, can be found at the back.

WAYLAND
www.waylandbooks.co.uk

OUR INCREDIBLE PLANET

Planet Earth is a very special place.
It is the only planet we know of
that has living things on it.

Earth is about
5 billion years old.

| = 1 billion years

Complete the
facts about
Earth with
stickers.

Ten per cent of Earth's
surface is ice.

It takes eight minutes and 20 seconds for light to travel from the Sun to Earth.

Earth is not perfectly round – it is a bit flat at the top and bottom.

More than 7 billion people live on Earth, and that number is getting bigger every day.

= 1 billion people

Seventy per cent of Earth's surface is covered in water. Only 30 per cent is land.

WATER, WATER EVERYWHERE

Stick these sea creatures in the correct part of the ocean. The deeper you go, the stranger they get.

Earth is sometimes called the 'blue planet' because the water on it makes Earth look blue from space. The water is full of life, but different creatures live in different parts of the sea.

The 'sunlit zone' is the closest to the surface, the brightest and warmest layer. Most of the sea's creatures live here.

Dolphin

Shark

Tuna

Flying Fish

Viper fish

Greenland shark

-200 metres

Lantern fish

Sperm whale

The water on Earth is split into five different areas, or 'oceans'.

Arctic Ocean

Indian Ocean

Atlantic Ocean

Southern Ocean

Pacific Ocean

Deep-sea anglerfish

The 'twilight zone' is dark and cold. Most of the creatures who live here have big eyes and teeth.

Colossal squid

The 'midnight zone' is pitch black and almost freezing. Few creatures live here.

Vampire squid

-1,000 metres

-4,000 metres

BOILING HOT

The hottest places on Earth are deserts — and the biggest of all is the Sahara desert, in Africa. The creatures who live there have to be very good at dealing with the heat.

Camels can drink between 100—150 litres of water in one go.

Dung beetles eat the poo of desert animals.

Naked mole rats keep out of the sun by living underground all the time.

I am one cool dude!

Temperatures can reach up to 50°C.

Silver ants are covered in fine silvery hairs that reflect the sunlight.

The horned viper snake wriggles sideways, keeping most of its body off the hot desert sand.

Fennec foxes keep cool by staying in their home during the day.

Stick these creatures in their sandy desert homes.

Jerboas do not need to drink — they get the water they need from their food.

FREEZING COLD

The coldest place on Earth is Antarctica. The temperature in the winter is usually about -60°C but the coldest temperature ever taken was -94°C!

Only one warm-blooded creature lives on land in the Antarctic during the cold winter months — the Emperor penguin.

Temperatures can drop to -60°C.

When I grow up I will be as tall as you!

Stick the egg on the penguin's feet so it can keep it warm.

Emperor penguins are the tallest penguins. They are 115 centimetres tall when fully grown — about the same height as you.

The Arctic is another very cold place. The temperature in winter is usually about -40°C. Animals that live here include reindeer, the arctic fox, the arctic wolf and polar bears.

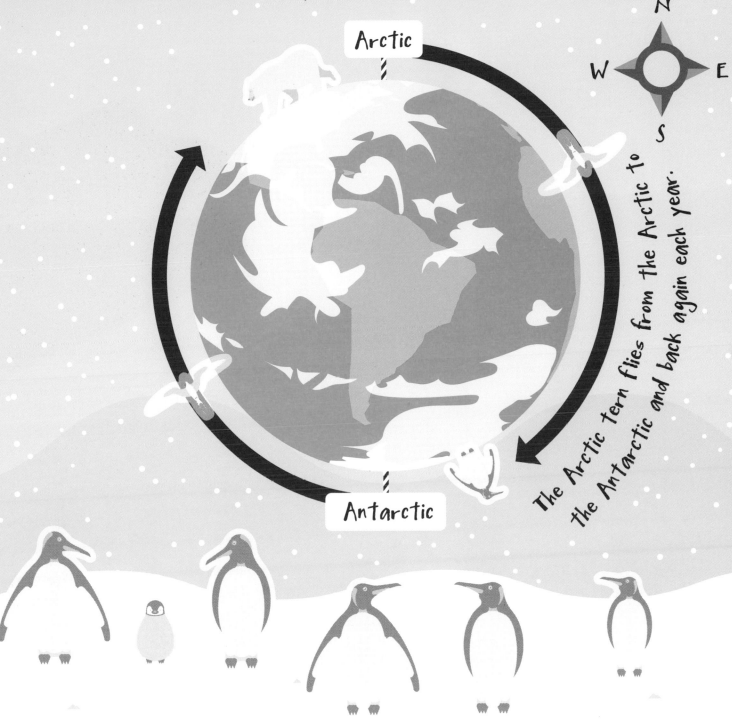

Arctic

N
W   E
S

The Arctic tern flies from the Arctic to the Antarctic and back again each year.

Antarctic

The Emperor penguin dad keeps the egg warm through winter while the mum searches for food. When the egg hatches, the mum comes back so the dad can look for food. Both parents look after the chick until it is about five months old and can swim and catch food for itself.

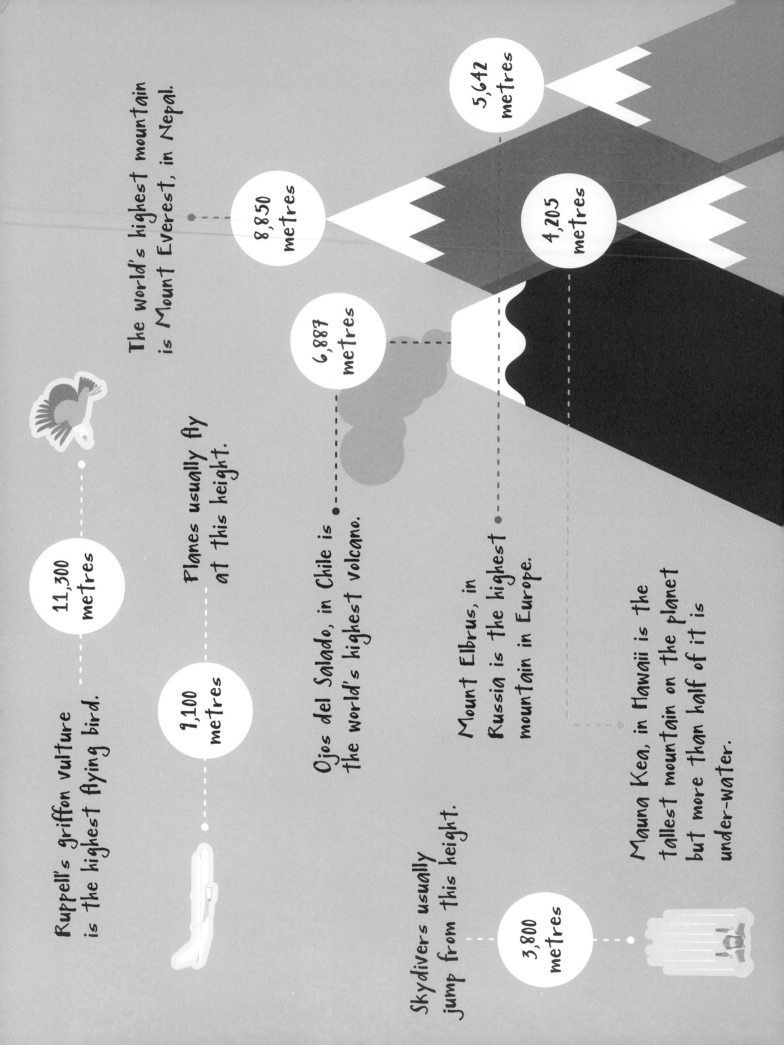

11,300 metres

Ruppell's griffon vulture is the highest flying bird.

9,100 metres

Planes usually fly at this height.

8,850 metres

The world's highest mountain is Mount Everest, in Nepal.

6,887 metres

Ojos del Salado, in Chile is the world's highest volcano.

5,642 metres

4,205 metres

Mount Elbrus, in Russia is the highest mountain in Europe.

Mauna Kea, in Hawaii is the tallest mountain on the planet but more than half of it is under-water.

Skydivers usually jump from this height.

3,800 metres

OCEAN DEEP, MOUNTAIN HIGH

From the top of a mountain to the bottom of an ocean, here are some of the highest and lowest places on the planet.

Stick the animals, people and vehicles at the right heights and depths.

-332 metres
The deepest a scuba diver has been to.

-2,992 metres
This is how deep a Cuvier's beaked whale can dive.

-3,800 metres
The wreck of RMS Titanic, which sank in 1912.

-10,908 metres
The deepest submarine dive ever by Deepsea Challenger in 2012.

-10,994 metres
The lowest place on the planet is the bottom of the Mariana Trench, in the Pacific Ocean.

There are more than 7 billion people living on Earth today. Some continents have more people living on them than others...

= 1 billion people.

NORTH AMERICA
360 million people

SOUTH AMERICA
410 million people

THE PEOPLE'S PLANET

The land on Earth is split into seven areas called 'continents'. They are: Asia, Africa, North America, South America, Europe, Oceania and Antarctica.

Show how many people live on each continent with the people stickers.

12

EUROPE
740 million people.

ASIA
4.4 billion people

Stick the animals and famous buildings on the continent they belong to.

OCEANIA
40 million people

AFRICA
1.2 billion people

ANTARCTICA
No one lives here but scientists visit to study it.

TOWERING ABOVE US

The Burj Khalifa in Dubai is the tallest building in the world. But it will be knocked into second place when the Kingdom Tower, in Saudi Arabia is finished. It will be 1,000 m — more than three times the height of the Eiffel Tower.

Kingdom Tower, Saudi Arabia

1,000 metres

Use your stickers to help finish building the Kingdom Tower.

Burj Khalifa, UAE

828 metres

Shanghai Tower, China

632 metres

Makkah Royal Clock Tower, Saudi Arabia

601 metres

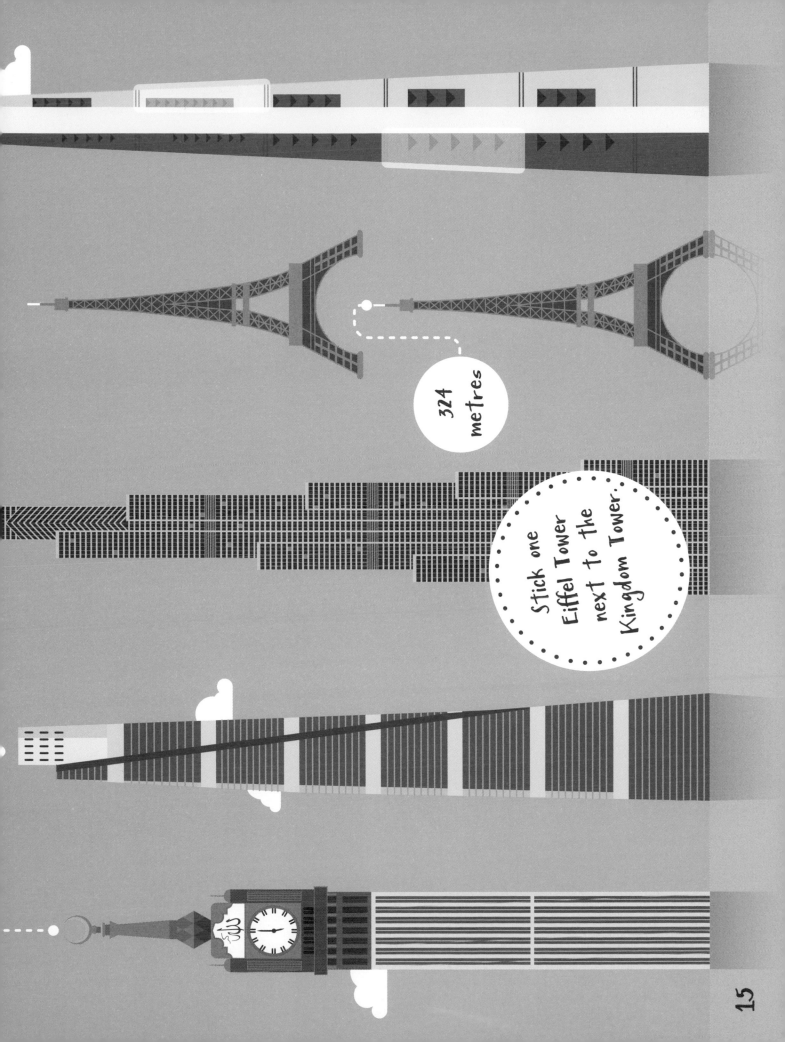

324 metres

Stick one Eiffel Tower next to the Kingdom Tower.

CITY UNDER THE SEA

The Great Barrier Reef is found in the warm, shallow waters off the coast of Australia. It is the largest coral reef in the world and is so big that astronauts can see it from space!

Stick the sea creatures on and around the reef.

Coral comes in all sorts of shapes and sizes. Some look like trees, flowers, mushrooms, fans, stars and even human brains!

There are five cheeky clownfish hiding — can you find them all? The answers are on page 32 if you need some help.

The reef is home to more than 400 types of coral and 1,500 types of fish, as well as whales and dolphins. It is like a busy, bustling city for sea creatures.

Help the reef grow by sticking different types of coral on the sea bed.

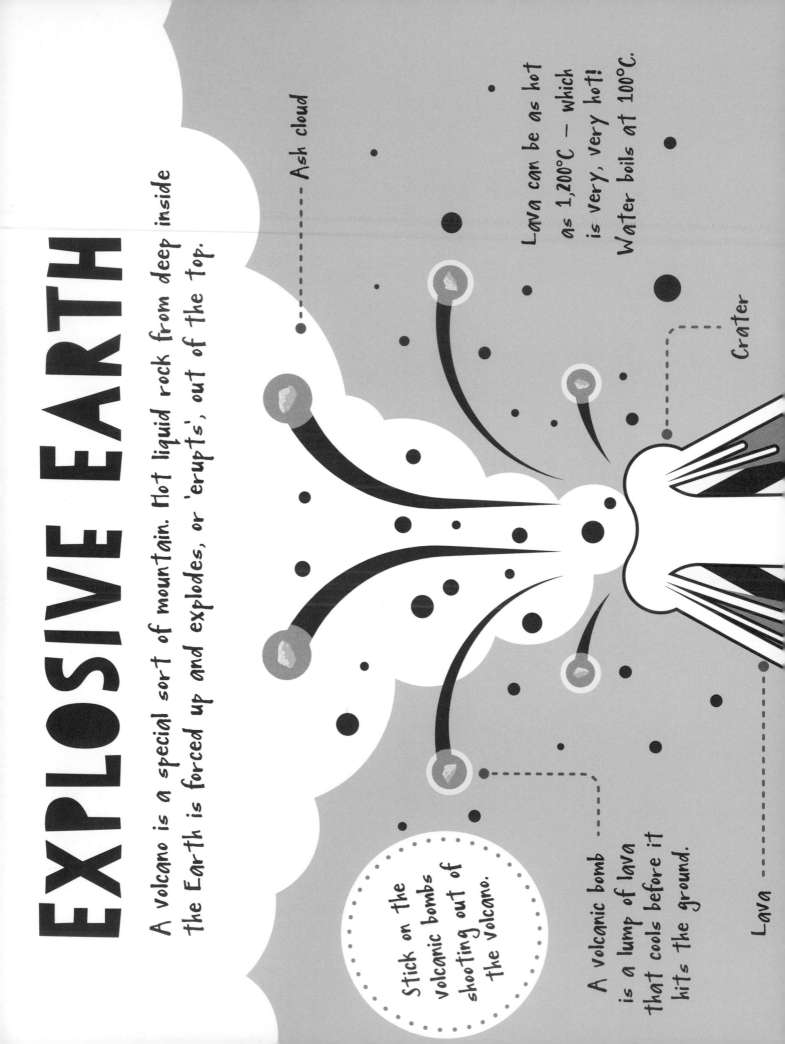

EXPLOSIVE EARTH

A volcano is a special sort of mountain. Hot liquid rock from deep inside the Earth is forced up and explodes, or 'erupts', out of the top.

Ash cloud

Lava can be as hot as 1,200°C — which is very, very hot! Water boils at 100°C.

Crater

Stick on the volcanic bombs shooting out of the volcano.

A volcanic bomb is a lump of lava that cools before it hits the ground.

Lava

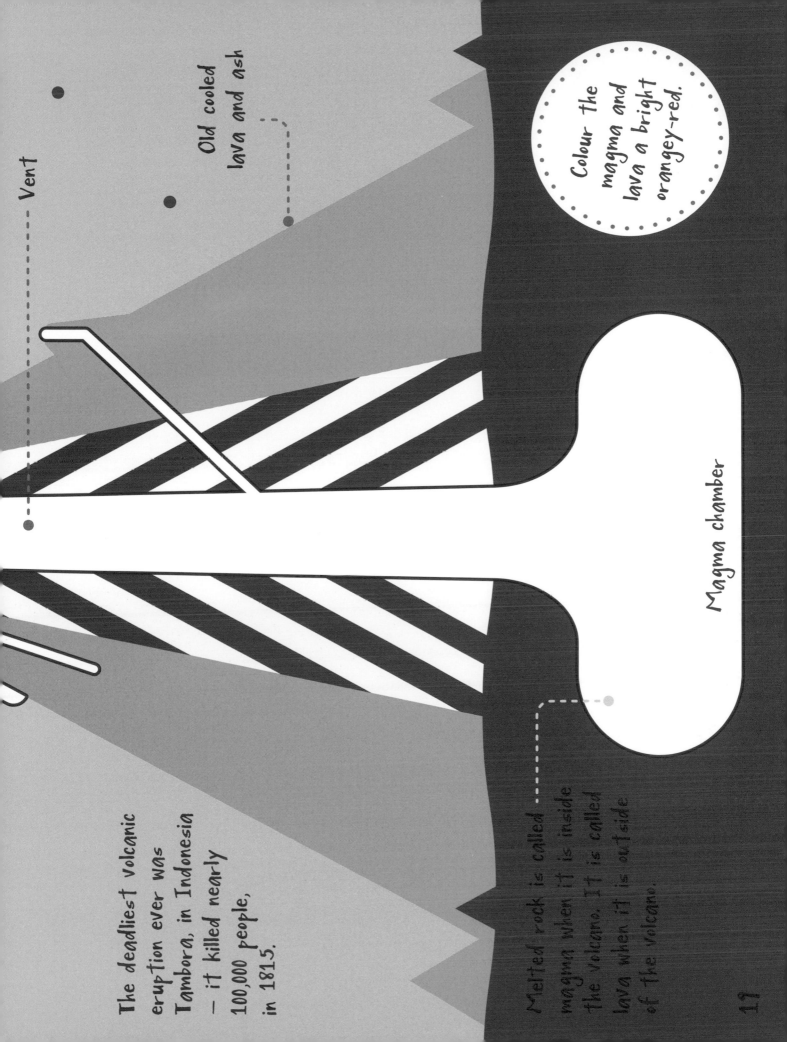

Vent

Old cooled lava and ash

Colour the magma and lava a bright orangey-red.

Magma chamber

The deadliest volcanic eruption ever was Tambora, in Indonesia — it killed nearly 100,000 people, in 1815.

Melted rock is called magma when it is inside the volcano. It is called lava when it is outside of the volcano.

19

HOME SWEET HOME

Hot, cold, rainy and windy weather means that some parts of the planet can be difficult places for humans to live. Here are some unusual buildings and shelters that people call home.

Igloos are built by Inuit (IN-yoo-it) people, who live in cold Arctic places. These dome-shaped shelters are made from large blocks of hard, dry snow.

Build these unusual homes out of stickers. Which one would you like to live in?

There are cave houses in Spain and Italy but the strangest are in Matmata, in Tunisia. Being in the hillside or the ground helps these homes stay cool in summer and warm in winter.

The Tuareg (TWAH-reg) people live in and around the Sahara desert in Africa. Their tents give them shade from the Sun and shelter from sandstorms.

People who live close to rivers sometimes build houses on legs so they do not get flooded. The Warao (wah-Row-oh) people live on the Orinoco river, in Venezuela. Their houses are on poles, with a roof but no walls.

INCREDIBLE JOURNEYS

Some animals make the most amazing journeys from one part of the planet to another, at the same time each year. This is called migration.

Wildebeest

Kenya

= 30,000 km

Tanzania

Wildebeest travel almost 30,000 kilometres across Africa, from the Serengeti National Park in Tanzania to the Maasai Mara National Reserve in Kenya.

Use stickers to show the animals migrating.

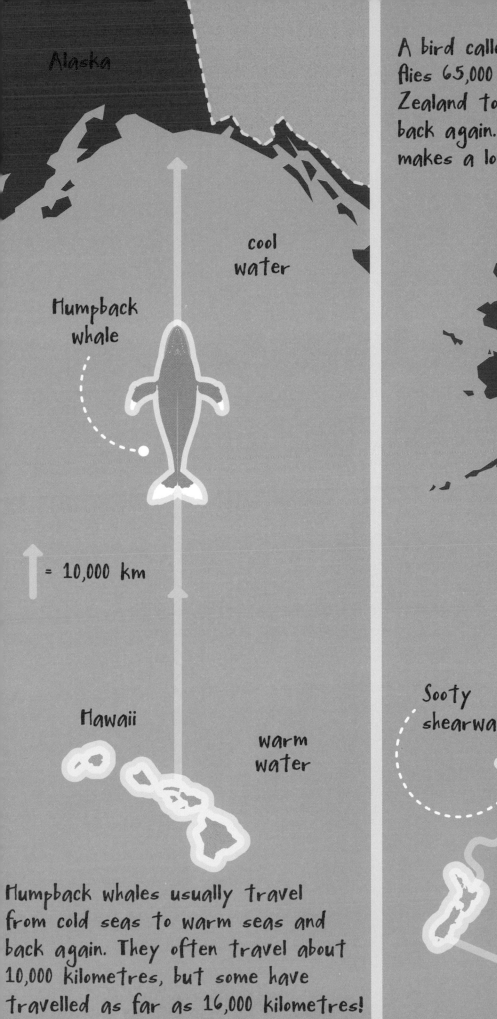

Alaska

cool
water

Humpback
whale

↑ = 10,000 km

Hawaii

warm
water

Humpback whales usually travel from cold seas to warm seas and back again. They often travel about 10,000 kilometres, but some have travelled as far as 16,000 kilometres!

A bird called the sooty shearwater flies 65,000 kilometres from New Zealand to the coast of Alaska and back again. Only the Arctic tern makes a longer migration in the sky.

Alaska

Sooty
shearwater

↑ = 65,000 km

New
Zealand

TREE HOUSE

Rainforests are warm, wet places packed full of life — and the Amazon rainforest in South America is the largest of all. Here are just a few of the creatures who live there.

Stick the animals in the correct layer of the rainforest.

Harpy eagle

Morpho butterfly

Macaw

60 metres

The emergent layer is sunny and includes the tallest trees.

40 metres

The canopy is where lots of animals live and the height of most of the trees in the rainforest.

Vampire bat

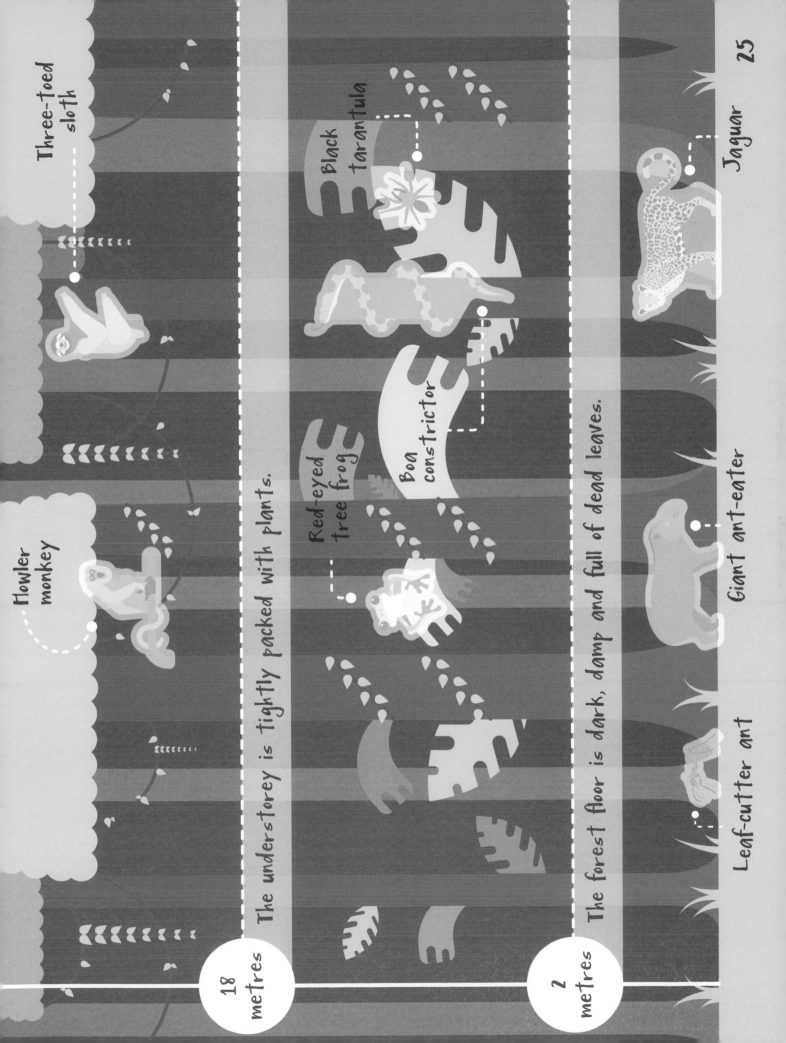

Three-toed
sloth

Black
tarantula

Jaguar

Howler
monkey

Red-eyed
tree frog

Boa
constrictor

Giant ant-eater

Leaf-cutter ant

18
metres

The understorey is tightly packed with plants.

2
metres

The forest floor is dark, damp and full of dead leaves.

WATER OF LIFE

A river is the path that fresh water takes as it travels to the ocean or sea. The longest river in the world is the Nile, in Africa. It flows through five countries, including Egypt.

Stick the animals in and around the River Nile.

Egyptian cobra

Ibis

Nile monitor lizard

Nile perch

The world's longest rivers:

Nile, Egypt 6,650 km

Amazon, Brazil 6,400 km

Yangtze, China 6,300 km

Mississippi, USA 6,275 km

Grey heron

Egyptian plover

Nile crocodile

Colour in the Nile crocodile and Egyptian plover.

WILD WEATHER

A tornado is a spinning tube of air that comes down from a storm-cloud and touches the ground. It is one of the most powerful types of weather.

Tornadoes can happen in most parts of the world but the USA has more than 1,000 every year.

A 'violent' tornado has a wind speed of more than 330 kilometres per hour. Powerful enough to pick up cars.

A 'strong' tornado has a wind speed of up to 250 kilometres per hour. Powerful enough to blow the roof off a house.

A 'weak tornado' has a wind speed of less than 180 kilometres per hour. This is powerful enough to snap a tree in half.

Stick in the objects that the tornado has picked up.

Not all weather destroys things, sometimes it can create something beautiful. A rainbow is made when sunlight shines through water in the air, such as raindrops or mist.

Add raindrop stickers and colour in the rainbow — make sure you get the colours in the right order. From the bottom going up, it should be red, orange, yellow, green, blue, indigo and violet.

PROTECTING

If you have read the rest of this book you will know how amazing our planet is. But some of the things we do are harmful to it.

The air around us is warming up because of the gases made by things like cars, aeroplanes, and factories.

Warmer weather means ice in the Arctic and Antarctic is melting, making it harder for the animals who live there to survive.

Our oceans are getting warmer and filling up with litter and chemicals. This is killing plants and sea creatures.

Trees in forests and jungles are being chopped down, causing flooding and leaving animals without a home.

OUR PLANET

The good news is, there are lots of things you can do to help. These things may seem small but if everyone did them it would make a real difference.

Switch off the lights and TV when you leave a room to use less energy.

Create less pollution by walking or riding your bike rather than travelling in a car.

Wear a jumper instead of turning up the heating to save energy.

Lots of old things can be made into new things, this is known as 'recycling'. You can recycle paper, plastic, clothes, glass and batteries.

Plant trees to help the environment and create new homes for animals.

PUZZLE ANSWERS

Did you find all of the clownfish? Here is where they were hiding ...

Pages 16–17

First published in 2016 by Wayland
© Wayland 2016
All rights reserved.
Written by Jo Dearden
Edited by Corinne Lucas
Illustration and design by Wild Pixel Ltd.
ISBN: 978 0 7502 9907 7
Printed in Malaysia
10 9 8 7 6 5 4 3 2 1
Wayland, an imprint of Hachette Children's Group
Part of Hodder & Stoughton
Carmelite House
50 Victoria Embankment
London, EC4Y 0DZ
www.hachette.co.uk
www.hachettechildrens.co.uk